A Benjamin Blog and his Inquisitive Dog Guide

Australia

Anita Ganeri

raintree
a Capstone company — publishers for children

Raintree is an imprint of Capstone Global Library Limited, a company incorporated in England and Wales having its registered office at 7 Pilgrim Street, London, EC4V 6LB – Registered company number: 6695582

www.raintree.co.uk
myorders@raintree.co.uk

Edited by Helen Cox Cannons and Tony Wacholtz
Designed by Steve Mead
Original illustrations © Capstone Global Library Limited 2015
Illustrated by Sernur ISIK
Picture research by Svetlana Zhurkin
Production by Helen McCreath
Originated by Capstone Global Library Limited
Printed and bound in China by CTPS

ISBN 978 1 406 29086 8
18 17 16 15 14
10 9 8 7 6 5 4 3 2 1

British Library Cataloguing in Publication Data
A full catalogue record for this book is available from the British Library.

Acknowledgements
We would like to thank the following for permission to reproduce photographs: Alamy: Jason Freeman, 16, National Geographic Image Collection, 21, Wildlight Photo Agency, 15; Dreamstime: Joern Schulz, 8, Ron Sumners, cover, Tamara Bauer, 6; Getty Images: Darrian Traynor, 18, Robin Smith, 7; iStockphotos: EdStock, 25, GCHaggisImages, 26, Shmenny50, 10; Newscom: AFP/William West, 24, Photoshot/World Pictures/Rick Strange, 14, Robert Harding/Ken Gillham, 17; Shutterstock: Beata Becla, 20, Dan Breckwoldt, 13, deb22, 9, fritz16, 19, Globe Turner, 28, Markus Gebauer, 23, Neale Cousland, 22, Qik, 12, Ralph Loesche, 4, Taras Vyshnya, 27, 29, worldswildlifewonders, 11; XNR Productions, 5.

Every effort has been made to contact copyright holders of material reproduced in this book. Any omissions will be rectified in subsequent printings if notice is given to the publisher.

Some words are shown in bold, **like this.** You can find out what they mean by looking in the glossary.

Contents

Welcome to Australia!

Hello! My name's Benjamin Blog and this is Barko Polo, my **inquisitive** dog. (He's named after ancient ace explorer, **Marco Polo**.) We have just got back from our latest adventure – exploring Australia. We put this book together from some of the blog posts we wrote on the way.

Map labels:

Melville Island

Arafura Sea

PAPUA NEW GUINEA

Timor Sea

Bathurst Island

● **Darwin**

Torres *Strait*

Cape York Peninsula

Great *Coral Sea*

Arnhem Land

Gulf of Carpentaria

Kimberley Plateau

INDIAN OCEAN

Tanami Desert

GREAT DIVIDING RANGE

Barrier Reef

PACIFIC OCEAN

Great Sandy Desert

Lake Mackay

O U T B A C K

Central Lowlands

GREAT

ARTESIAN

BASIN

Gibson Desert

Macdonnell Ranges

Simpson Desert

Western Plateau

Lake Eyre

Great Victoria Desert

● **Brisbane**

● **Gold Coast City**

Darling River

Nullarbor Plain

Lake Gairdner

Lake Torrens

Lachlan River

GREAT DIVIDING RANGE

● **Perth**

DARLING RANGE

Great Australian Bight

Murray River

● **Newcastle**

● **Sydney**

● **Wollongong**

● **Adelaide**

● **Canberra**

Kangaroo Island

▲ Mt. Kosciuszco

Tasman Sea

N
W E
S

● **Melbourne**

AUSTRALIAN ALPS

0   200   400 mi.
0   200   400 km

Bass Strait

● **Hobart**

Tasmania

INDIAN OCEAN

| Major highways |

BARKO'S BLOG-TASTIC AUSTRALIA FACTS

Australia is a huge island that is also a country. It's surrounded by the Indian and Pacific Oceans. It makes up most of the **continent** of Australia, which is the smallest continent in the world.

The story of Australia

Posted by: Ben Blog | 5 September at 9.43 a.m.

We arrived in Australia and headed straight to Tasmania, an island off the south-east coast. We're visiting the old prison at Port Arthur. This is where criminals were sent from Britain in the 1800s. It's surrounded by shark-infested waters, so the prisoners had no chance of escape.

BARKO'S BLOG-TASTIC AUSTRALIA FACTS
In 1860, Robert Burke and William Wills led the first expedition across Australia. They died on the way back, here at Cooper Creek, from **starvation** and disease.

Rocks and reefs

Posted by: Ben Blog | 10 September at 8.07 p.m.

From Tasmania, we headed right into the middle of Australia to see Uluru (it used to be called Ayers Rock). It's a massive block of **sandstone** and a **sacred** place for the Indigenous Australians. We arrived here at sunset when the rock was glowing red. What a sight!

BARKO'S BLOG-TASTIC AUSTRALIA FACTS

The Great Barrier Reef runs for more than 2,000 kilometres (1,243 miles) along the north-east coast and is the world's biggest **coral reef**. It's home to thousands of animals – more than 1,500 types of fish, for a start.

After we left Uluru, we thought we'd explore some more of the outback. It's covered in sandy and stony deserts and is one of the hottest, driest places on Earth. I'm here in the Simpson Desert looking for Big Red, a famous **sand dune**. It's thirsty work.

BARKO'S BLOG-TASTIC AUSTRALIA FACTS

This amazing animal is a duck-billed platypus. It lives in rivers and streams in eastern Australia. The duck-billed platypus uses its webbed feet for swimming. It scoops up worms and shellfish from the muddy riverbed with its leathery, duck-like bill.

City sights

Posted by: Ben Blog | 28 September at 9.59 a.m.

Most Australians live in cities around the coast. Our next stop was Sydney, the biggest city in Australia. It's home to 4.5 million people and is a busy, lively place. Barko took this snap of me outside the Sydney Opera House, one of the most famous landmarks in the city.

BARKO'S BLOG-TASTIC AUSTRALIA FACTS

Canberra is the capital city of Australia. It was built from scratch in 1913. This is Parliament House where the Australian government meets. It was built in the shape of a **boomerang**.

G'day!

Many Australians have **ancestors** from Britain and Europe. Many other people have moved to Australia from New Zealand, China, India, Italy and Vietnam. The people in this photo are Indigenous Australians. They were the first people to live in Australia around 50,000 years ago.

BARKO'S BLOG-TASTIC AUSTRALIA FACTS

Most Australians speak English but with an Australian **accent** and their own words. I've been learning a few. "G'day" means "hello", "fair dinkum" means "that's true", and "ripper" means "great" or "fantastic".

In Australia, the school day usually lasts from 9 a.m. until 3.30 p.m. Most children wear uniforms, and need sunhats and suncream all summer. Some children who live deep in the Australian outback cannot get to school. They have to have their lessons by radio or online instead.

BARKO'S BLOG-TASTIC AUSTRALIA FACTS

People in the Australian outback often live a long way from hospital, so they call a flying doctor instead. The Royal Flying Doctor Service has around 60 planes and flies tens of thousands of kilometres every day.

We're in the city of Melbourne for Australia Day. It's when Australians remember the arrival of the first ships from England. People are cheering and waving Australian flags, as they wait for the parade to pass. Later, there's going to be a spectacular firework display in Docklands.

BARKO'S BLOG-TASTIC AUSTRALIA FACTS

The Indigenous Australians believe in a time called the Dreaming when their **ancestors** made the world. They remember this time with dance and music. This man is playing a traditional Indigenous Australian instrument called the **didgeridoo**.

Time for a barbie

It had been a long day and we were hungry, so we headed down to the beach for a barbie (barbeque). Barko couldn't wait to sink his teeth into some juicy snags (sausages). I stuck to prawns and a burger, with **pavlova** for dessert.

20

BARKO'S BLOG-TASTIC AUSTRALIA FACTS

Bush tucker is food found in the wild. The Indigenous Australians in the outback lived off it for thousands of years. Fancy tucking into goanna (lizard), honey ants or witchetty grubs? They're all on the bush tucker menu.

Mad about sport

Posted by: Ben Blog | 15 March at 2.30 p.m.

Staying in Melbourne, we've come to the Melbourne Cricket Ground to watch a game of Australian (Aussie) rules football. Players can kick, punch or pick up the ball, but throwing is not allowed. We're cheering for Hawthorn – one of Melbourne's top teams.

BARKO'S BLOG-TASTIC AUSTRALIA FACTS
Many Australians live near the sea, so swimming and surfing are very popular. There are brilliant surfing beaches around the country, like this one at Bells Beach. Surf's up, so I'm heading in.

From cattle stations to opal mines

From Melbourne, we made our way west to the state of South Australia. We're spending a few days at Anna Creek cattle station, training to be jackaroos (cowboys). They've got around 17,000 cattle here. We'll be using trail bikes to round them up. Yikes!

BARKO'S BLOG-TASTIC AUSTRALIA FACTS

Shimmering gemstones called opals are one of Australia's most precious **natural resources**. They're mined here in Coober Pedy, a town in the Australian outback. It gets so hot in Coober Pedy that many people have also dug themselves homes underground.

And finally ...

The last stop on our tour was beautiful Rottnest Island off the coast of Western Australia. I wanted to see some quokkas. They are small, furry animals, about the size of cats. Quokkas are **marsupials**, like kangaroos and wallabies, and they're very rare. Here's a snap I took.

I am here!

BARKO'S BLOG-TASTIC AUSTRALIA FACTS

This is Sydney Harbour Bridge. It's nicknamed "the coathanger" because of its arch shape. You can climb to the top for a breathtaking view of the city, but you'll need a good head for heights.

Australia fact file

Area: 7,692,024 square kilometres
(2,969,907 square miles)

Population: 23,371,900 (2014)

Capital city: Canberra

Other main cities: Sydney, Melbourne, Brisbane

Language: English

Main religion: Christianity

Highest mountain: Mount Kosciuszko
(2,228 metres/7,310 feet)

Longest river: Murray River
(2,508 kilometres/1,558 miles)

Currency: Australian dollar

Australia quiz

Find out how much you know about Australia with our quick quiz.

1. What is Uluru made from?
a) opals
b) limestone
c) **sandstone**

2. What does "ripper" mean?
a) fantastic
b) rubbish
c) sunny

3. What is a **didgeridoo**?
a) an Australian drink
b) an Australian animal
c) an Australian musical instrument

4. What sport do Hawthorn play?
a) cricket
b) Aussie rules football
c) rugby

5. What is this?

5. Sydney Harbour Bridge
4. b
3. c
2. a
1. c
Answers

Glossary

accent way of speaking and pronouncing words

ancestor relative from the past

boomerang wooden, V-shaped object that was thrown for hunting

continent one of seven huge areas of land on Earth

coral reef long structure made from coral that grows along the coast

didgeridoo long, pipe-like musical instrument

inquisitive interested in learning about the world

Marco Polo explorer who lived from about 1254 to 1324. He travelled from Italy to China.

marsupial mammal with a pouch in which its babies grow

natural resource natural material that we use, such as coal, oil or wood

pavlova dessert made from meringue, topped with fruit and cream

sacred another word for holy, or special, to a person's religion or beliefs

sand dune giant heap of sand found in deserts and on beaches, piled up by the wind

sandstone soft rock that can be red, brown or grey

starvation death caused by lack of food

Find out more

Books

Australia (Countries Around the World), Mary Colson (Raintree, 2012)

Australia (Discover Countries), Chris Ward (Wayland, 2013)

Australia: Everything you ever wanted to know (Not For Parents) (Lonely Planet, 2013)

Websites

kids.nationalgeographic.co.uk/kids/places/find
National Geographic's website has lots of information, photos and maps of countries around the world.

www.kids-world-travel-guide.com/australia-facts.html
This website contains interesting Australia facts that have been chosen and researched by children especially for other children.

www.worldatlas.com
Packed with information about different countries, this website has flags, time zones, facts and figures, maps and timelines.

Index